Plant Based Diet for Beginners

50 Healthy Plant Based Recipes

AUTHOR: TUPAKULA

Table of Content

Introduction

Previously like Hollywood celebrities I accompanied alkaline, juice and smoothie weight loss plan's to maintain lean body with controlled weight, balancing the pH value in body, and to keep away from a few fitness and health problems like heart, liver, arthritis diseases and sicknesses, however how an awful lot ever I do physical games and comply with the weight loss plan I confronted some troubles and felt concerned in lowering stubborn stomach fat and body weight, then after detail research and seeing consequences I followed new healthy weight loss program known as **PLANT BASED DIET**, you would possibly listen to it however didn't try it, Actually it is similar to paleo, vegan diet's.

At first, congratulations for selecting and downloading Plant Based Diet Recipes book to maintain good and lean body with fewer fats, these recipes ensure you cut your fat content in the body by increasing energy, health, and vitality. Coming to facts, there are many exceptional gains of advantages of the plant-based diet plan, but due to lack of knowledge, the lot of people missing secure manner to maintain and keep lean body with full energy and disposing of fats from the body to hold healthy life for a long time.

There are different ways to prepare yummy, mouthwatering and nutritious plant-based recipes than just adding bunches of ingredients in the meal. So, to avoid this, clearly explained in different chapters and each chapter will explain each and necessary steps taken to follow and make plant-based recipes including macro nutritional details like protein, fat, and carbohydrates.

Additionally, you will analyze distinctive sorts of beneficial tips and tricks to ensure that your dietary habits will develop as quickly as possible, including how to totally commit to the food regimen.

After that, you will discover 50 best plant-based recipes which will manipulate you to get a lean body without losing energy and vitality levels in 30 days with inclusive smoothie's recipes. This recipe is one of the best ways to achieve your dreams to get a lean body in less period of time with increased health.

The key to start a new diet correctly is doing whatever you could within your power with clear mind to reduce your weight and to get lean body by following a complete plant-based diet, for any successful regimen in your life are reminder, routine and reward yourself with additional energy bar, smoothie or juice while you accomplished your weekly target for greater health.⊠

CHAPTER 1:
Why Plant Based Diet & It's Benefits

The plant-based diet is a low-fat, high carb and protein diet that has similar qualities like vegan, paleo, and raw food diets. Frequently, required energy for the body collected from glucose or erythritol.

Why plant-based diet: Plant-based diet allows easy absorption of nutrients straight into the bloodstream and helps to heal the body and digestive system very fast and aids in weight control but meat items will slow down the digestive system.

Fresh greens: Most people will think about frozen food to make quickly, but remember fresh greens are always going to be healthier than frozen items. Prepare them first and freeze them until you are ready to use it, this will be the best way to use and keep your body healthier.

Protein myth: Plants contain 30 to 40 percent of greens are a great source of protein in the body, which provide protein in the form of amino acids and building blocks of protein. This makes the body to utilize them easier than other animal products and easier for the digestive system. If you feel that you required additional protein for your body due to heavy workouts, feel free to add protein powder in your mixer while making juice.

Eating vegetables and natural products as a major aspect of our day to day life will help to overcome some genuine medical issues. Most fruits and vegetables are normally low in fat and calories but fruits have low fat and more fiber and water, this makes digestive system healthy because fruits have low sodium-content with natural erythritol.

Fruits and vegetables will have some similar nutrients, micronutrients are a class of supplements that incorporate vitamins, minerals, and phytonutrients that are essential for the body to maintain the proper healthy functioning of the organs.

Leafy vegetables have more micronutrients than any other vegetables or fruits like iron, calcium, and magnesium. Which play a key role in the proper functioning of the nervous system as well as the immune system.

Root vegetables are the powerhouses of minerals, vitamins and also additionally supply carbohydrates, especially complex-carbohydrates, which gradually supply constant energy to the body.

If you feel that you required additional protein for your body due to heavy workouts, feel free to add plant-based protein powder in your food or juices or smoothies, while making yummy and delicious plant-based recipes (some of the plant-based protein powder are pea protein powder, hemp protein powder, soy protein powder, brown rice protein powder, pumpkin protein powder).

CHAPTER 2:
Brief Overview of Plant Based Food

When you start eating plant-based food, automatically body starts losing weight immediately, and you will feel and look better from the inside out. Some of the health benefits you will achieve while eating include:

Weight loss: After trying plant-based recipes, you will be surprised to learn that this recipe is one of the best ways to get lean body without any difficulty because this recipe contains high quantity of water filled with green leafy veggies with high fiber content, which helps you stay full for a long time and also reduce cravings for junk food

Rich nutrient: Mostly prefer unprocessed food, when you cook any food for a long time in high temperature, it will destroy many nutrients, but in case of plant-based food all ingredients are raw and fully loaded with vitamins, minerals, antioxidants, water, fiber, phytonutrients, anti-inflammatory substances, and chlorophyll. This chlorophyll has a similar structure to hemoglobin in blood, which acts as cleansing blood transfusion

Easy to digest: The plant-based foods contain more valuable nutrients than any other food items like meat and take less time to digest, this is because body spends, the more effort of energy in the digestion process so your body doesn't have to. These food recipes contain high quantity of phytonutrients, which keeps your digestive system functioning properly and improves health by reducing future diseases

Detoxification: Normally our body tries to eliminate toxins from our body, but due to lack of organic food, it will slow down the body's detoxification system and causes weight gain, we have to thank plant-based foods because it will produce fiber, which helps you in cleansing your digestive system and eliminate toxins

Hydration: Normally, staying hydrated gives energy and helps your brain, immune system, and digestive system work properly without any defects. Simple way to check yourself whether you are hydrated or dehydrated by looking at your urine color, if it is strong yellow color, then you are dehydrated that means our body directly saying that we forgot to drink sufficient water due to our busy work, in this case, we have to thank green juices because it contains 70% of water and avoids us from dehydration, now you will start realizing the advantages of greens in your life

Blood sugar improvement: Blood erythritol levels will be improved because it reduces glucose and glycated hemoglobin in the body

Blood sugar growth: Researchers identified that diet will lead to lower the blood pressure in overweight or obese individuals and helps to reduce strokes and heart diseases

Cholesterol problems: Helps to reduce the bad cholesterol and increases good cholesterol, which is necessary for the body

Acne: Recent human studies have shown a drastic drop in acne lesions and skin inflammation over 10-12 weeks

Energy: This makes and also gives your body more reliable energy which keeps your body more energizes during a day

Anti-aging: When you start eating plant-based food, you can see changes not only inside but also outside of the body, especially after toxin free slowly it will start eliminating wrinkles, acne and dark circles under eye and makes your face young again

Highly portable: Plant-based foods can be prepared in less time (10 minutes) and makes your dream come true, which can be stored for a long time in a cool place but immediate consumption will give best results

Great option to replace meat: When you think about meat replacement, one of the best and great option is plant-based items, which are homemade and also low fat delicious shakes, packed with protein and fiber, which makes you to not eat junk food in between meals.

I can explain most numerous health benefits of plant-based foods, but you are going to learn more information as we go through this book and you will discover excellent health benefits yourself, once again thank you for downloading the book and enjoy each and every recipe you encounter and this book makes you make your own recipes for good health.

CHAPTER 3:
Plant Based Recipes

Breakfast Recipes

Recipe 1: Pistachio Roasted Pears

Ingredients

- Pears 5
- Cinnamon powder 1 tsp.
- Cumin seeds 1 tsp.
- Pistachio 4 tsp. (crushed)
- Cashews 4 tsp.
- Ginger stem 1 tbsp.

Preparation Method

1. At first, preheat your oven to 180ºC. Boil (2 minutes) and cut the pears then place on oven-proof form then sprinkle cinnamon and place in oven for 20 minutes or until they brown only at the edges, let cool down.
2. Now, toast the pistachio and cashews in oven for 5 minutes, save few roasted cashews serving.
3. Now blend pears, ginger stem, roasted nuts until quite smooth then divide the pear mixture into 4 parts.
4. Finally, decorate with chopped roasted cashews, cumin seeds and serve immediately to enjoy delicious taste.

Nutritional Information

- Preparation Time: 50 minutes
- Total servings: 4
- Calories: 171 (per serving)
- Fat: 8.4g
- Protein: 3.9g
- Carbs: 24.2g

Recipe 2: Fresh Berry Oats

Ingredients
- Vegetable butter 1 tsp.
- Oats 1 cups
- Oats milk 1 cup
- Water 2 cups
- Stevia 2 tbsp.
- Lemon zest 1 tbsp.
- Fresh berries 4 oz.
- Flax seeds ¼ cup
- Coconut flakes 2 tbsp.
- Cinnamon for extra taste

Preparation Method
1. At first, place your pot in medium heat and add vegetable butter. When butter is melted, add oats and toast, constantly stir until it smells nutty, ca, 1 to 2 minutes.
2. Add oats milk, water, stevia, lemon zest, and cook for 10 minutes then stir oats, berries and flax seeds.
3. Cover and let sit 5 minutes until oats comes to desired thickness. Finally, top with additional berries, cinnamon, coconut flakes, and enjoy the taste.

Nutritional Information
- Preparation Time: 15 minutes
- Total Servings: 2
- Calories: 221 (per serving)
- Fat: 5.2g
- Protein: 8.3g
- Carbohydrates: 30.6g

Recipe 3: Avocado Slice Bread

Ingredients
- Vegetable butter ½ tsp.
- Sesame bread 1
- Sliced large avocado ½
- Fresh lemon juice 2 tsp.
- Cucumber slices 2
- Tomato slices 2
- Himalayan salt to taste
- Black pepper to taste

Preparation Method
1. At first, splits and toast the sesame bread and apply vegetable butter.
2. In a small bowl, add avocado with the lemon juice, salt, and pepper then divide evenly, spread on bread with the avocado mixture and top with the cucumber slices, tomato to enjoy the extra delicious taste.

Nutritional Information
- Preparation Time: 5minutes
- Total servings: 1
- Calories: 367 (per serving)
- Fat: 14.6g
- Protein: 11g
- Carbs: 37g

Recipe 4: Fennel Vegetable Tortilla

Ingredients

- Fennel slices 2
- Pepper slices 2
- Tortilla 1 halved
- Hummus ¼ cup
- Parsley 2 tbsp.
- Olives 2 tbsp.
- Olive oil 2 tsp.
- Pink salt to taste
- Black pepper to taste
- Fresh lemon juice 1 tbsp.

Preparation Method

1. In a medium bowl, combine the fennel, peppers, parsley, olives, lemon juice, olive oil, salt and pepper.
2. Shaped sandwiches with pita, hummus, vegetables and enjoy the taste.

Nutritional Information

- Preparation Time: 10 minutes
- Total servings: 1
- Calories: 378 (per serving)
- Fat: 8.1g
- Protein: 11.5g
- Carbs: 32.5g

Recipe 5: Miller Berry Pancakes

Ingredients
- Ground flax seeds 1 tbsp.
- Vegetable butter 1 tbsp.
- Soy milk ½ cup
- Millet flour 1 cup
- Cranberries 2 oz.
- Cold water 2 tbsp.
- Baking powder 1 tsp.
- Virgin oil 1 tbsp.
- Himalayan sea salt to taste
- Maple syrup for extra flavor
- Soy yogurt for extra flavor

Preparation Method
1. At first, whisk flax seeds in cold water, then set aside to thicken. Meanwhile, the melt vegetable butter in a small pan over a medium heat then let.
2. Now, combine soy milk and add to the melted butter then whisk in the flax seeds mixture.
3. Combine the flour, baking powder, salt, gradually pour in the wet mixture, with constant stirring until it combined. Fold the cranberries, and set aside.
4. Preheat oven at low temperature then heat a splash of virgin oil in a large frying pan over a medium heat. Add a scoop of dough in the pan then add more scoop of dough, ensuring that it is nicely round shape.
5. Deeply cook each side for 2 minutes and place in the oven to keep warm while making remaining pancakes.
6. Serve with soy yogurt, maple syrup, and extra cranberries if desired to enjoy the taste.

Nutritional Information
- Preparation Time: 20 minutes
- Total servings: 4
- Calories: 184 (per serving)
- Fat: 7g
- Protein: 6.9g
- Carbs: 25.6g

Recipe 6: Crusted Vegetable Pots

Ingredients

Crust:

- Ghee 2 tbsp.
- Almond flour 4 oz.
- Coconut flour 2 oz.
- Baking powder 2 tsp.
- Himalaya salt ¼ tsp.
- Dried dill ¼ tsp.
- Mozzarella cheese 2 oz.

Filling:

- Ghee 2 tbsp.
- Vegetable mix 1 lb.
- Red onions 1 oz.
- Vinegar 1 tbsp.
- Paprika 2 tsp.
- Pink salt to taste
- Pepper to taste

Preparation Method

1. At first, preheat your oven to 350F then grease your muffin or cupcakes with ghee.
2. Now, we can make filling by placing pan over medium heat and add ghee. When ghee is hot add diced vegetables and cook until it roasted.
3. Add remaining all ingredients and cook for 15 minutes then keep aside.
4. Now you can start making crust, by mixing all crust ingredients one by one in log shape. It should be soft then divide it into 12 equal parts.
5. Roll each piece and place two rolls on each other than press over muffin tins.
6. Now, fill the muffins cups with cooled filling and top with one more roll.
7. Finally place in preheated oven and cook for 25 minutes or until you find golden brown on top of muffins.
8. Let it cool for 5 minutes and enjoy the taste with your family.

Nutritional Information

- Preparation Time: 45 minutes
- Total servings: 4
- Calories: 454 (per serving)
- Fat: 3.4g

- Protein: 12.1g
- Carbs: 31.6g

Recipe 7: Cabbage Chia Bread

Ingredients

Bread:
- Ghee 1 tbsp.
- Chia flour 7 oz.
- Pumpkin spice 2 tsp.
- Baking soda ¼ tsp.
- Lemons zest 1 tbsp.
- Erythritol 3 oz.
- Cinnamon 1 tsp.
- Cabbages puree 5 oz.

Topping:
- Erythritol 1.5 oz.
- Cinnamon ½ tsp.
- Lemons zest 1 tbsp.
- Pinch of salt

Preparation Method

1. At first, preheat your oven to 300F. In a large bowl, add chia flour, cinnamon, pumpkin spice, baking soda and mix well and add ghee, Erythritol, cinnamon and mix well.
2. Add a spoon of cabbages puree and mix well (fresh puree gives better taste then canned).
3. Now, add juice and zest half of a lemon and mix. In another bowl, prepare the cheesecake topping by mixing all topping ingredients.
4. Spoon the bread batter into a baking dish suitable for bread and distribute evenly using a ladle. Add a layer using half of the cheese mixture on top of the bread batter and spread evenly.
5. Mix the remaining cheese mixture with the cabbages puree. Gently spoon the cabbage cheese mixture on top and spread evenly. Transfer into the preheated oven and bake for 60 minutes, make sure that bread is not going to burnt on top.
6. Carefully remove from the baking dish, slice into 12 pieces and enjoy the taste.

Nutritional Information

- Preparation Time: 80 minutes
- Total servings: 12
- Calories: 309 (per serving)

- Fat: 3.3g
- Protein: 9.9g
- Carbs: 25.4g

Lunch Recipes

Recipe 8: Broccoli Pepperoni Rice

Ingredients

- Ghee 2 tbsp.
- Broccoli rice 1 lb.
- Pepperoni 8.5 oz.
- Jalapeno peppers 3 oz.
- Dry red chili 1
- Turnip greens 2 tbsp.
- Rosemary 1 tbsp.
- Allspice 1 tsp.
- Salt and pepper to taste

Preparation Method

1. At first, grate broccoli and make rice from it. Keep aside.
2. On other side, slice pepperoni, jalapeno peppers, dry red chili and keep aside.
3. Now, place a large skillet over medium heat and add ghee. When ghee is hot, add peppers, chili, allspice, turnip greens and pepperoni. Cook until slightly browned.
4. Add the broccoli rice and cook for 10 minutes, season with salt, pepper. Add finely chopped rosemary and enjoy the taste.

Nutritional Information

- Preparation Time: 20 minutes
- Total servings: 4
- Calories: 379 (per serving)
- Fat: 3.3g
- Protein: 9.9g
- Carbs: 21.5g

Recipe 9: Green Coated Beans

Ingredients

- Vegetable oil 2 tbsp.
- Green beans 1.5 lb.
- Garlic 3 cloves
- Nuts 1 oz. (your choice)
- Groundnut powder 1 tbsp.
- Herbs 1 tbsp.
- Salt and pepper to taste

Preparation Method

1. At first, place a large pot of salt water to boil over medium heat then add the green beans and cook until tender, about 3-4 minutes.
2. Now, heat the vegetable oil in a large skillet over medium heat then add chopped garlic cloves, nuts and cook for 2-3 minutes.
3. When green beans are cooked, drain and place on the pan. Add ground nut powder, salt, pepper and toss to coat.
4. Finally, transfer coated green beans to a bowl with sprinkled herbs and enjoys the delicious taste.

Nutritional Information

- Preparation Time: 15 minutes
- Total servings: 6
- Calories: 151 (per serving)
- Fat: 3.6g
- Protein: 5.6g
- Carbs: 14.5g

Recipe 10: Yummy Tempeh with Kale

Ingredients

- Vegetable oil 2 tbsp.
- Turmeric ¼ tsp.
- Tomatoes 3 oz.
- Tempeh ½ lb.
- Scallions 3
- Kale 4 oz.
- Lemon juice 2 tsp.
- Herbs 1 tbsp.
- Cayenne pepper ½ tsp.
- Pink salt and pepper to taste

Preparation Method

1. In medium bowl, mix tempeh, black pepper, salt, cayenne and set aside.
2. Place a pan over medium heat and add vegetable oil, scallion and cook until it looks soft then add tempeh mixture and stir well until tempeh turns to brown color, approximately 4-5 minutes.
3. Now, add kale, lemon juice, tomatoes and pink salt and cook for 1 minute. Turn of the heat and add chopped herbs over it to enjoy the delicious taste.

Nutritional Information

- Preparation Time: 25 minutes
- Total servings: 2
- Calories: 311 (per serving)
- Fat: 5.2g
- Protein: 15.9g
- Carbs: 16.9g

Recipe 11: Green Lentil Salad

Ingredients
- Vegetable oil 2 tbsp.
- Spring onions ½ cup
- Green lentils 7 oz.
- Tomatoes 4 oz.
- Parsley 1 bunch
- Mixed herbs 2 tbsp.
- Lemon juice 2 tbsp.
- Pink salt ½ tsp.
- Black pepper to taste

Preparation Method
1. At first, rinse the lentils then boil in the salt water until it is tender then drain and allow cooling.
2. Meanwhile, trim and finely chop the spring onions, halve the tomatoes, then parsley and herb leaves.
3. Finally, mix the chilled lentils with spring onions, tomatoes, herbs, vegetable oil, lemon juice, zest, season with salt and black pepper and then serve to enjoy yummy herb salad taste.

Nutritional Information
- Preparation Time: 25 minutes
- Total servings: 4
- Calories: 292 (per serving)
- Fat: 4.5g
- Protein: 12.7g
- Carbs: 27.2g

Recipe 12: Caper Herb Pasta

Ingredients
- Vegetable oil 1 tbsp.
- Pasta ¾ lb.
- Chickpeas 15 oz.
- Capers ¼ cup (flinders rose)
- Garlic cloves 2
- Ginger powder ½ tsp.
- Pink salt to taste
- Fresh black pepper to taste
- Fresh herbs ½ cup
- Fresh lemon juice 2 tbsp.

Preparation Method
1. At first, preheat your oven to 400°F. Cook the spaghetti according to the given instructions on packet then drain and put in the pot.
2. Meanwhile, mix chickpeas, capers, vegetable oil, garlic, ginger, pink salt, pepper then place in oven and roast for 15 minutes or until it becomes crispy.
3. Finally, add roasted chickpeas mixture, lemon juice and chopped herbs to the pasta and toss to combine. If desired, add little spicy sauce and enjoy the taste.

Nutritional Information
- Preparation Time: 35minutes
- Total servings: 4
- Calories: 332 (per serving)
- Fat: 4g
- Protein: 10.8g
- Carbs: 32.5g

Recipe 13: Kimchi Almond Bowl

Ingredients
- Kimchi 2 oz.
- Black sesame seeds 1 tsp.
- Almond flakes 3 tbsp.
- Chili flakes 1 tsp.
- Broccoli 4 oz.

Sauce:
- Tahini 2 tbsp.
- Lemon juice 3 tbsp.
- Chili sauce 3 tbsp.
- Cayenne pepper 1 tsp.

Preparation Method
1. At first, combine sauce ingredients in a small bowl then stir until smooth and creamy (add more water to thin if desire).
2. Now, place the kimchi in bowls then top with sauce, black sesame seeds, almond flakes and chili flakes.
3. Finally, enjoy the yummy bowl with delicious taste.

Nutritional Information
- Preparation Time: 15 minutes
- Total servings: 2
- Calories: 384 (per serving)
- Fat: 2.5g
- Protein: 5.9g
- Carbs: 12.2g

Recipe 14: Winter Vegetable Stew

Ingredients

- Vegetable butter 2 tbsp.
- Winter vegetable mix 1 lb.
- Garlic powder 1 tsp.
- Ginger powder 1 tsp.
- Tomato puree 1.5 oz.
- All spice 1 ½ tbsp.
- Paprika 1 ½ tsp.
- Pink salt to taste
- Diced tomatoes 7 oz.
- Coconut milk 1 cup
- Coriander 1 ½ tbsp.
- Herbs 2 tbsp.

Preparation Method

1. At first, mix chopped winter vegetables into bite sized pieces and season with pink salt, pepper and garlic, ginger and mix well.
2. Add canned diced tomatoes and tomato paste, mix well again then add coconut milk and mix well.
3. Cook for 35 minutes on medium heat. Before serving, add vegetable oil, chopped herbs and enjoy extra flavor taste.

Nutritional Information

- Preparation Time: 40 minutes
- Serving per Recipe: 5
- Calories: 266.8 (per serving)
- Fat: 6.6g
- Protein: 9.2g
- Carbs: 33.3g

Recipe 15: Avocado Arugula Bowl

Ingredients

- Ghee 1 tbsp.
- Arugula 1 cup
- Brussels sprouts 1 cup
- Avocado ½ piece (sliced)
- Red chili sauce 1 tbsp.
- Mint 2 tbsp.
- Sunflower seeds 1 tbsp.
- Pink salt to taste
- Pepper to taste

Preparation Method

1. At first, sauté sprouts for approximately 15 minutes or until lightly browned and tender then slice half avocado.
2. Finally, in a large bowl place arugula, mint, sprouts avocado, sunflower seeds as a layer and enjoy the yummy taste.

Nutritional Information

- Preparation Time: 20 minutes
- Total servings: 2
- Calories: 311 (per serving)
- Fat: 20.6g
- Protein: 10.7g
- Carbs: 5g

Recipe 16: Coconut Potato Stew

Ingredients

- Vegetable oil 2 tsp.
- Onions 2 oz.
- Potatoes ½ lb.
- Broccoli 5 oz.
- Dry tomatoes 2
- Coconut milk 1 cup
- Turmeric 1 tsp.
- Allspice 1 tsp.
- Chili powder ¼ tsp.
- Water 1 cup
- Herbs 1 tbsp.
- Himalayan salt to taste
- Fresh pepper to taste

Preparation Method

1. Heat in a large skillet pan; add vegetable oil and onions over medium heat. Cook about 5 minutes.
2. Add potatoes, broccoli to the pan and brown. Season with salt, pepper, allspice, chili powder, turmeric and mix well.
3. Add coconut milk, dry tomatoes and water. Reduce heat to simmer about 30 minutes or until desired taste comes. Before serving, sprinkle with chopped herbs and enjoy the taste.

Nutritional Information

- Preparation Time: 35 minutes
- Total servings: 4
- Calories: 377 (per serving)
- Fat: 5.1g
- Protein: 15.1g
- Carbs: 32.7g

Recipe 17: Vegetable Quiche

Ingredients

Crust
- Vegetable mix 5 oz.
- Coconut flour 5 oz.
- Chia meal 3 tbsp.
- Pink salt ½ tsp.

Filling
- Ghee 1 tbsp.
- Heavy whipping cream 4 fl oz.
- Spring onions 1 oz.
- Cream cheese 3 oz.
- Asparagus spears 8 oz.
- Pink salt to taste
- Pepper to taste
- Fennel for garnish

Preparation Method

1. At first, preheat the oven to 400F. Put vegetables into a food processor or blender and make powder.
2. Add powdered vegetable in a mixing bowl together with the coconut flour and chia meal, pink salt and mix until well combined.
3. Now, mix the dough using hand or hand mixer, place this dough in a rectangular baking tray with removable bottom (30 x 20 cm / 12 x 8 inch).
4. Bake in preheated oven for 15 minutes and keep aside until it cools down. Reduce the oven to 350F.
5. Meantime, take a large bowl and add the cream, season with salt and pepper and whisk until it combines well
6. On the other hand, place a pan over medium heat with ghee. When ghee is hot, add sliced spring onions and cook for 3 minutes or until fragrant. Add the mixture and combine well. Add cream cheese to the mixture.
7. Now, top the mixture with asparagus and place in preheated oven for 30 minutes or until lightly browned and crispy on top.
8. Garnish with freshly chopped fennel and enjoy the taste.

Nutritional Information

- Preparation Time: 60 minutes
- Total servings: 8
- Calories: 410 (per serving)

- Fat: 6g
- Protein: 14.4g
- Carbs: 33.5g

Dinner Recipes

Recipe 18: Tamari Soy Squash

Ingredients

- Vegetable oil 1 tbsp.
- Spaghetti squash 1 lb.
- Cauliflower 1 cups
- Kale 2 oz.
- Tempeh 0.5 lb.
- Tamari 1 tbsp.
- Soy sauce 1 oz.
- Allspice 1 tsp.
- Noodle sauce 1 lb.
- Parsley 1 tbsp.

Preparation Method

1. At first, preheat your oven to 375°F. In medium bowl, mix tempeh, tamari, allspice and set aside for 30 minutes.
2. Cook squash halves for 30 minutes and set aside. Now add vegetable oil in a large pan over medium heat and fry tempeh mixture for 5 minutes, add remaining ingredients such as sauce, cauliflower, kale and boil for 5 minutes.
3. Finally, add to serving plate and sprinkle chopped parsley to enjoy yummy taste.

Nutritional Information

- Preparation Time: 45 minutes
- Total servings: 4
- Calories: 401 (per serving)
- Fat: 9.1g
- Protein: 20.1g
- Carbs: 27.7g

Recipe 19: Vegetable Mixed Beans

Ingredients
- Vegetable oil 1 tbsp.
- Spring onions ¼ cup
- Tomatoes 10 oz. (diced)
- White beans 15 oz.
- Kidney beans 15 oz.
- Allspice 2 tsp.
- Fresh herbs 1 cup
- Roasted garlic 3 cloves
- Water 2 cups
- Black pepper to taste
- Pink salt ½ tsp.
- Soy yogurt for extra taste

Preparation Method
1. At first, heat vegetable oil in a large pot over medium heat and add spring onions and cook until tender, about 3-4 minutes.
2. Now, add tomatoes, water, pink salt, pepper and bring to a boil. After 3 minutes, add the white beans, kidney beans and cook until heated, about 5 minutes.
3. In a small bowl, mix roasted garlic, herbs, vegetable oil and salt. Divide cooked beans under the individual bowls and top with the soy yogurt. Serve with the bread to enjoy the extra yummy taste.

Nutritional Information
- Preparation Time: 20 minutes
- Total servings: 3
- Calories: 408 (per serving)
- Fat: 6.5g
- Protein: 11.4g
- Carbs: 41.9g

Recipe 20: Fried Red Leeks

Ingredients
- Vegetable oil 2 tbsp.
- Leeks 20
- Red vinegar 2 tbsp.
- Fresh herbs 1 tbsp.
- Allspice 1 tsp.
- Salt water (for boiling)

Preparation Method
1. At first, preheat your oven to 400°F. Remember 5 leeks per person, depending on their size you are using.
2. Now, easily cut both ends and peel back the first or second layer of leek leaves then boil in a pan with salt water for 2 minutes.
3. Drain and mix with vegetable oil, red vinegar, chopped herbs, and allspice. Evenly spread the leeks in a layer on a baking tray and cook for about 10 minutes in the oven until it caramelizes.

Nutritional Information
- Preparation Time: 20 minutes
- Total servings: 4
- Calories: 79 (per serving)
- Fat: 2g
- Protein: 2.9g
- Carbs: 5.5g

Recipe 21: Forest Broccoli Bowl

Ingredients

- Ghee 1 tbsp.
- Broccoli 2 oz.
- Forest mushrooms 1 lb.
- Nuts ½ tbsp.
- Coriander 2 cups
- Ginger paste 21 tsp.
- Lemon juice 1 tbsp.
- Himalayan salt to taste
- Pepper to taste

Preparation Method

1. At first, soak nuts overnight in water then drain water and add nuts, coriander, ginger, lemon juice, salt, and pepper to food processor then process until smooth.
2. Now, cook broccoli in small pan over medium heat for 10 minutes and keep aside then place large skillet over medium heat with ghee and add forest mushrooms, season with salt and pepper then cook for 10 minutes, don't forget to stir occasionally until all the water has evaporated and they begin to brown and keep aside.
3. Finally, add broccoli, a quarter of the forest mushrooms and top with a tablespoon of the pesto in bowl and enjoy the delicious taste.

Nutritional Information

- Preparation Time: 35 minutes
- Total servings: 4
- Calories: 231 (per serving)
- Fat: 4.4g
- Protein: 8.3g
- Carbs: 21g

Recipe 22: Green Sauced Linguine

Ingredients

- Vegetable oil 1 tbsp.
- Kale 1 oz.
- Olives 4
- Capers 2 oz.
- Pepper flakes ¼ tsp.
- Tomato sauce 20 oz.
- Herbs ½ cup
- Lemons juice 1 tsp.
- Linguine (noodles) 1 lb.
- Almonds 1 oz. (chopped)

Preparation Method

1. At first, heat the olive oil over medium heat then add red pepper to skillet until fragrant, approximately some seconds.
2. Now, add the tomato sauce, kale, olives, capers, herbs, lemons juice and cook on simmer for 15 minutes.
3. Meanwhile, cook the linguine according to the instructions given on packet and pour the sauce over linguine and top with chopped almonds to enjoy the yummy taste.

Nutritional Information

- Preparation Time: 20 minutes
- Total servings: 4
- Calories: 436 (per serving)
- Fat: 7.1g
- Protein: 12.3g
- Carbs: 37.6g

Recipe 23: Sweet Broccoli Bowl

Ingredients
- Cauliflower rice 2 (cooked)
- Sweet potatoes 2 (cubed & roasted)
- Broccoli heads 2 (roasted)
- Green lentil 20 oz. (cooked)
- Kimchi 2 cups
- Chili flakes 1 tsp.
- Mixed herbs 2 tbsp.

Sauce:
- Allspice 1 tsp.
- Miso 1 tbsp.
- Tahini 2 tbsp.
- Lemon juice 2 tbsp.
- Soy sauce 1 tbsp.
- Water 3 tbsp.

Preparation Method
1. At first, combine sauce ingredients in a small bowl then stir until smooth and creamy (add more water to thin if desire).
2. Now, place the sweet potatoes, cauliflower rice, broccoli, green lentil, and kimchi in bowls then top with herbs and chili flakes.
3. Finally, enjoy the yummy buddha broccoli bowl with delicious taste.

Nutritional Information
- Preparation Time: 5 minutes
- Total servings: 4
- Calories: 388 (per serving)
- Fat: 4.2g
- Protein: 8.8g
- Carbs: 35.2g

Recipe 24: Mixed Squash Salad

Ingredients

- Vegetable oil 2 tbsp.
- Fresh tomato 1
- Butter squash 1 oz.
- Acorn squash 1 oz.
- Yellow squash 1 oz.
- Turnip greens 1 tbsp.
- Fresh thyme 1 ½ tbsp.
- Vinegar 1 tbsp.
- Fresh black pepper to taste
- Himalaya salt to taste

Preparation Method

1. In a food processor, put chopped fresh basil, turnip leaves with oil to make the paste.
2. Slice tomato into 1/4" slices. You should be able to get at least 6 slices from the tomato and squash's.
3. Assemble salad by layering tomato, squash and paste.
4. Season with salt, pepper, and remaining oil and enjoy the taste.

Nutritional Information

- Preparation Time: 12 minutes
- Serving per Recipe: 2
- Calories: 239 (per serving)
- Fat: 3.1g
- Protein: 9.9g
- Carbs: 26.6g

Recipe 25: Coconut Cauliflower Stew

Ingredients

- Vegetable oil 2 tsp.
- Onions 2 oz.
- Garlic powder 1 tsp.
- Ginger powder 1 tsp.
- Cauliflower 1 lb.
- Coconut milk 1 cup
- Parsley 1 tbsp.
- Cumin powder 1 tsp.
- Green chili 1 tsp.
- Turmeric 1 tsp.
- Tomato sauce 1 oz.
- Pink salt to taste
- Fresh pepper to taste

Preparation Method

1. Heat in a large skillet pan; add oil and onions on medium heat. Cook about 10 minutes. Add garlic and ginger, cook for another 2 minutes.
2. Add cauliflower to the pan and brown. Season with salt, pepper, cumin, coriander, green chili, turmeric and mix well.
3. Add coconut milk, tomato sauce and water. Reduce heat to simmer about 20 minutes and simmer for an additional 15 minutes or until desired taste comes.

Nutritional Information

- Preparation Time: 35 minutes
- Total servings: 4
- Calories: 255 (per serving)
- Fat: 3.6g
- Protein: 10.2g
- Carbs: 28g

Recipe 26: Ghee Soy Balls

Ingredients

Meatballs
- Vegetable oil 1 tbsp.
- Ground soy 0.5 lb.
- Onions 1 oz.
- Garlic cloves 2
- Flax meal 1 oz.
- Coconut milk 1 tbsp.
- Salt to taste

Coconut Broth
- Coconut milk 2 oz.
- Broth 2 oz.

Spices
- Coriander seeds 1 tsp.
- Turmeric ½ tsp.
- Cinnamon ½ tsp.
- Red pepper ½ tsp.
- Ginger powder ½ tsp.
- Garlic powder ½ tsp.
- Chili paste 1 tsp.

Preparation Method

1. In a large pan, add oil. When oil is hot, add garlic, onions and cook until fragrant and translucent.
2. Meantime, combine flax meal, coconut milk, ground soy, salt and create a paste.
3. Add onions, garlic to this paste and create small balls using hand. Place the pan over medium heat and add ghee. When ghee is hot add soy balls all over the pan (ca. 15 minutes).
4. When soy balls is browned on both sides, add coconut milk, broth, and all spices, mix well and cook for 20 more minutes.
5. Finally, serve with some coconut broth with soy balls in a bowl and enjoy the taste.

Nutritional Information

- Preparation Time: 30 minutes
- Total servings: 2
- Calories: 442 (per serving)

- Fat: 6.1g
- Protein: 13.4g
- Carbs: 36.4g

Soup Recipes

Recipe 27: Yummy Watermelon Soup

Ingredients
- Fresh tomatoes 2 cups
- Fresh watermelon 2 cups
- Fresh red peppers 2
- Red onions ¼ cup
- Lime juice 1 tbsp.
- Allspice 1 tsp.
- Herbs ¼ cup
- Pink salt ½ tsp.

Preparation Method
1. At first, place tomatoes, watermelon, red pepper, onions in a pan and blender until thoroughly pureed.
2. Add the remaining ingredients except herbs, blend to combine. Cook for 60 minutes in simmer and serve with herbs for yummy taste.

Nutritional Information
- Preparation Time: 60 minutes
- Total servings: 4
- Calories: 180 (per serving)
- Fat: 1.2g
- Protein: 5.1g
- Carbs: 15g

Recipe 28: Super Cucumber Soup

Ingredients

- Tomatoes 2
- Cucumber 1
- Onion ½ cup
- Green pepper ½ piece
- Vegetable stock 2 cups
- Garlic clove 1
- Vinegar 1 tbsp.
- Pepper sauce 2 tsp.
- Pink salt ¼ tsp.
- Chili powder 1 tsp.

Preparation Method

1. At first, in a large bowl mix all ingredients and cook for 30 minutes over medium heat.
2. Let it cool for 10 minutes and serve to enjoy spicy soup taste.

Nutritional Information

- Preparation Time: 40 minutes
- Total servings: 2
- Calories: 55 (per serving)
- Fat: 0.5g
- Protein: 2.8g
- Carbs: 8g

Recipe 29: Ground Green Soup

Ingredients
- Olive oil 1 tbsp.
- Spring onions ½ cup
- Celery sticks 2
- Fresh kale ½ lb.
- Leek 1
- Fresh peas 4 oz.
- Garlic cloves 2
- Potatoes 3
- Zucchinis 2
- Vegetables broth 4 cups
- Fresh herbs 1 tbsp.
- Pink salt to taste
- Pepper to taste
- Allspice 1 tsp.

Preparation Method
1. At first, place a large sauce pan over medium heat and add chopped spring onions, celery, leeks, garlic, olive oil and vegetable broth, close the lid and cook for 15 minutes.
2. Meanwhile cut potatoes, zucchinis in 2 cm chunks and put in sauce pan. Now, add pinch of pink salt, allspice and pepper for better taste and continue to cook for another 15 minutes or until the potato is boiled properly.
3. Now, add the peas and the kale and cook for 5 more minutes. Using blender, blend the mixer until smooth. Check once the taste and add salt and pepper, if desired.
4. Finally, add chopped mint leaves, discard the stalks and enjoy deliciously soup.

Nutritional Information
- Preparation Time: 40 minutes
- Total servings: 8
- Calories: 125 (per serving)
- Fat: 2.5g
- Protein: 5.5g
- Carbs: 13.7g

Recipe 30: Purple Cabbage Soup

Ingredients

- Vegetable oil 1 tbsp.
- Garlic cloves 2
- Vegetable broth 1 cup
- Water 1 cup
- Purple cabbage 4 oz.
- Coconut milk 2 tbsp.
- Pink salt to taste
- Pepper to taste
- Paprika 1 tsp.
- Herbs 1 tbsp.

Preparation Method

1. Place a large soup pot over medium heat and add oil. When oil is hot add chopped garlic and cook until translucent.
2. Now, add broth, water and boil for 15 minutes. Season with salt, pepper, and paprika.
3. Meanwhile, cut cabbage into small florets and add to soup, reduce the heat to low and cook for 20 minutes.
4. Once the cabbage is cooked, add shredded cheese's, coconut milk and turn off the heat and serve in serving bowl and sprinkle herbs then mix well.

Nutritional Information

- Preparation Time: 45 minutes
- Total servings: 2
- Calories: 198 (per serving)
- Fat: 3.3g
- Protein: 7.6g
- Carbs: 21.2g

Recipe 31: Green Pumpkin Soup

Ingredients
- Vegetable oil 2 tbsp.
- Onions 1 cups
- Ginger 1 tbsp.
- Green chili 1
- Garlic cloves 2
- Pink salt 1 ½ tsp.
- Vegetable broth 4 cups
- Tomato puree 2 cups
- Acorn pumpkin 1 (small chunks)
- Black peas 16 oz.
- Curry leaves 1 tsp.
- Allspice 1 tsp.

Preparation Method
1. At first, heat the oil in a pan over medium heat then add the onions and cook for 5 minutes then add the ginger, chili, garlic, salt, cumin and cook for 2 more minutes.
2. Now, add the broth, tomato puree, acorn pumpkin and cook until the pumpkin is tender, about 30 minutes.
3. Finally, add the black peas, allspice and cook for 5 minutes. Using blender, blend mixture into smooth puree.
4. Before serving sprinkle with chopped curry leaves for extra taste.

Nutritional Information
- Preparation Time: 50 minutes
- Total servings: 4
- Calories: 236 (per serving)
- Fat: 3g
- Protein: 9.1g
- Carbs: 38g

Recipe 32: Fresh Broccoli Bay Soup

Ingredients
- Vegetable oil 1 tbsp.
- Vegetable broth 1 ½ cups
- Bacon 4 slices
- Broccoli puree 1 cup
- Garlic 1 tsp.
- Ginger 1 tsp.
- Red chili flakes 2
- Fresh ginger ½ tsp.
- Mint ¼ tsp.
- Bay leaf 1
- Himalayan salt ½ tsp.
- Pepper ½ tsp.
- Dry herbs 1 tbsp.

Preparation Method
1. Keep saucepan over medium heat, add oil. When oil is hot, add garlic and fresh ginger.
2. Let this sauté for about 3 minutes or until onions start to go translucent then add spices (salt, pepper, coriander, bay leaf, red chili flakes) to the pan and let cook for 2 minutes. Add broccoli puree to pan and stir into the onions and spices well
3. Once the broccoli is mixed well, add vegetable broth to the pan. Stir until everything is combined.
4. Bring to a boil to simmer for 20 minutes. Once simmered, use an immersion blender to blend together all of the ingredients. You want a smooth puree here so make sure you take your time. Cook for an additional 20 minutes.
5. Crumble the dry herbs over the top of the soup and enjoy the taste of the soup.

Nutritional Information
- Preparation Time: 45 minutes
- Serving per Recipe: 3
- Calories: 245 (per serving)
- Fat: 4.1g
- Protein: 8.8g
- Carbs: 31.7g

Recipe 33: Chili Bean Soup

Ingredients
- Olive oil 2 tbsp.
- Bulgur ½ cup
- Water 3 cup
- Onions ½ cup
- Green peppers 1
- Garlic cloves 2
- Chili powder 1 tsp.
- Tomatoes 14 oz. (diced)
- White beans 15 oz.
- Shallots 2 (chopped)
- Jalapeno 1(chopped)
- Himalayan salt 1 tsp.
- Black pepper to taste
- Herbs ½ cup

Preparation Method
1. At first, bring 1 cup of water to boil then add bulgur and cook until all the water is absorbed and the bulgur is tender, approximately 12 to 15 minutes.
2. Meantime, heat olive oil in a pot over medium heat and add onions, pepper and cook until tender, approximately 8 minutes.
3. Now, add garlic, green pepper, chili powder, Himalayan salt, pepper and cook until fragrant. Add tomatoes and 2 cups of water. Bring to a boil and add beans until slightly thickened, approximately 10 minutes.
4. Add shallots, jalapeno, remaining ghee, salt and pepper in the bulgur then divide the chili under the bowls and above with the bulgur and sprinkled herbs.

Nutritional Information
- Preparation Time: 40 minutes
- Total servings: 4
- Calories: 339 (per serving)
- Fat: 5g
- Protein: 11.1g
- Carbs: 39g

Dessert Recipes

Recipe 34: Fresh Rosemary Pears

Ingredients
- Fresh pears 3
- Lemon juice ¼ cup
- Cinnamon ¼ tsp.
- Fresh rosemary 1 tbsp.
- Erythritol ¼ cup

Preparation Method
1. At first, cut the pears and the wedges then spread the wedges on dessert plates. Pour the lemon juice over pear wedges.
2. Combine the rosemary, erythritol, cinnamon and sprinkle over the pears to enjoy the delicious taste.

Nutritional Information
- Preparation Time: 10 minutes
- Total servings: 4
- Calories: 98 (per serving)
- Fat: 0.3g
- Protein: 1g
- Carbs: 21g

Recipe 35: Yummy Watermelon Mint

Ingredients
- Watermelon 1 lb.
- Fresh mint ½ bunch
- Lime juice 1 tbsp.
- Lime zest 1 tbsp.
- Erythritol ¾ cup

Preparation Method
1. At first, cut the watermelon into 2-inch thick rounds and cut each in 4 wedges.
2. In a medium bowl, add chopped mint leaves, lime zest, erythritol and mix well.
3. Finally, place the watermelon on a serving plate; squeeze the lime juice over the wedges, sprinkle mint lime erythritol over it and enjoy the taste.

Nutritional Information
- Preparation Time: 10 minutes
- Total servings: 6
- Calories: 86 (per serving)
- Fat: 0.2g
- Protein: 1.1g
- Carbs: 21g

Recipe 36: Honey Chia Cakes

Ingredients

- Vegetable oil 1 oz.
- Chia meal 1 cup
- White chocolate 2 oz.
- Erythritol 4 tsp.
- Honey 1 oz.
- Pink salt ¼ tsp.
- Baking soda 1 tsp.
- Nut powder 1 oz.

Preparation Method

1. At first, preheat your oven to 350F. In small bowl, add erythritol, vegetable oil, honey and mix well.
2. In separate bowl, combine all chia meal, white chocolate, nut powder, baking soda and pink salt.
3. Mix bowl1 and bowl2 mixture using hand mixer then place batter into a 10x8 baking pan and bake for 20 minutes.
4. Let brownies cakes cool and slice it into 8 equal parts and enjoy eating while drinking coffee or tea.

Nutritional Information

- Preparation Time: 30 minutes
- Total servings: 8
- Calories: 102 (per serving)
- Fat: 3.2g
- Protein: 7.7g
- Carbs: 15.7g

Recipe 37: Walnut Apple Cake

Ingredients

- Vegetable oil 1 oz.
- Apples 3
- Erythritol 7 oz.
- Buckwheat flour 1 cup
- Baking powder 1 tsp.
- Allspice 1 tsp.
- Lemon juice 1 tsp.
- Lemon zest 1
- Walnuts 3 oz.
- Water ½ cup

Preparation Method

1. At first, preheat your oven to 180°C and grease cake mold with oil.
2. Slice the 2 apples and keep aside. Mix erythritol and melted oil in a pan, then add to cake mold and top with the apple slices in a single layer.
3. Now, mix buckwheat flour, erythritol, baking soda and mixed spices in a bowl. In another separating bowl, combine the oil, water, lemon juice, grated 1 apple and lemon zest. Mix the dry ingredients with the wet, quick, but thorough.
4. Chop the walnuts roughly then pour over the apple layer in the cake mold and bake for 30 minutes or until a spit comes out clean.
5. Allow the cake to cool for 5 minutes and enjoy the taste.

Nutritional Information

- Preparation Time: 45 minutes
- Total servings: 9
- Calories: 220 (per serving)
- Fat: 5.4g
- Protein: 6.8g
- Carbs: 39.6g

Recipe 38: Cocoa Flax Brownies

Ingredients
- Vegetable butter 1 tbsp.
- Cocoa powder 2 oz.
- Flaxseed powder 6 tbsp.
- Water 9 tbsp.
- Beans 14 oz. (make paste)
- Erythritol 8 oz.
- Ground almonds 2 oz.
- Baking powder 1 tsp.
- Fruit extract 1 tsp.
- Chocolate 3.5 oz.

For coconut cream:
- Coconut Cream 8 fl oz.
- Erythritol 3 tbsp.
- Fruit extract ½ tsp.

Preparation Method
1. At first, before you make brownies, put your coconut cream in the refrigerator for 24 hours. Preheat the oven to 180°C, apply vegetable butter to brownie tins or plate and set aside.
2. In a small bowl, mix flaxseed powder with water, stir well and allow thickening on one side.
3. Add beans paste, erythritol, cocoa, ground almonds, baking soda, fruit extract to the flaxseed mixture and mix until you get shiny dough.
4. Now, cut the chocolate into small pieces then add to mixture. Spoon the dough in the prepared brownie tin and bake for 60 minutes.
5. In a small bowl, beat the chilled coconut cream, erythritol and fruit extract until thick and creamy paste.
6. Cut the brownie in squares and serve with the coconut cream to enjoy yummy taste.

Nutritional Information
- Preparation Time: 70 minutes
- Total servings: 9
- Calories: 280 (per serving)
- Fat: 5g
- Protein: 11g
- Carbs: 37g

Ingredients

Cake:
- Cream cheese 3 oz.
- Cream of tartar 2 tsp.
- Erythritol 2 oz.
- Cranberries 6 pieces

Frosting:
- Vegetable oil 1 oz.
- Cream cheese 1 lb.
- Erythritol mix 1 oz.
- Cranberries extract 1 tsp.
- Lemon juice 1 tbsp.

Preparation Method

1. At first, preheat your oven to 300 F. Spray 2 muffin tins with ghee then in a medium bowl, beat cream cheese, cranberries extract, sweetener until smooth.
2. In a separate bowl, whip cream of tartar with an electric mixer until stiff peaks form. Next, carefully fold the whipped cream into the yolk mixture.
3. Scoop about two tablespoons of the mixture into each muffin tin and gently press single cranberries into it then place in preheated oven and bake for 30 minutes or until golden brown.
4. Once done, remove the cake from the muffin tins and place on a cooling rack. While the cakes are cooling, combine all frosting ingredients together in a medium bowl.
5. Beat with an electric mixer until smooth. Transfer frosting to pastry bag with wide tip. Set aside 3 layers for each cake and then pipe frosting in between each layer of cake.

Nutritional Information

- Preparation Time: 45 minutes
- Total servings: 6
- Calories: 347 (per serving)
- Fat: 3.2g
- Protein: 7.2g
- Carbs: 14.1g

Snack Recipes

Recipe 40: Banana Bombs

Ingredients
- Vegetable butter 4 oz.
- Bananas 5
- Cream 4 oz.
- Vanillas extract 1 tsp.
- Stevia 10 drops
- Plant protein powder 1 tbsp.

Preparation Method
1. At first, mix butter and cream. Using a mixer, mix all the ingredients together or place in microwave oven for 30 seconds to 1 minute to soften them.
2. Add banana, vanilla extract and liquid stevia to the mixture and mix with a spoon.
3. Distribute the mixture into a silicone tray and freeze for 3 hours.

Nutritional Information
- Preparation Time: 182 minutes
- Total servings: 5
- Calories: 51 (per serving)
- Fat: 0.6g
- Protein: 3g
- Carbs: 9g

Recipe 41: Energy Peanut Bars

Ingredients

- Coconut butter 1 cup
- Pumpkin purees 1 cup
- Cinnamon 1 tbsp.
- Peanuts 1 oz.
- Peanut butter 3 oz.
- Plant protein powder 2 oz.
- Vegetable oil 2 tbsp.

Preparation Method

1. Hold aside 8x8 inch square baking tray with aluminum foil. In the large bowl, add melted coconut butter, peanut butter, pumpkin puree, spices, plant protein powder and mix well.
2. Add ghee and combine well without lumps. Pour the mixture into the already prepared pan and spread evenly then sprinkle chopped peanuts.
3. Cover with wax paper and evenly put into the pan. Remove wax paper and place the mixture in the refrigerator for 3 hours.
4. Use a sharp knife to cut into 25 equal squares and enjoy the delicious taste.

Nutritional Information

- Preparation Time: 15 minutes
- Total servings: 25
- Calories: 117 (per serving)
- Fat: 4.9g
- Protein: 11.7g
- Carbs: 15.6g

Recipe 42: Protein Flax Bars

Ingredients
- Flax ½ cup
- Vegetable butter 2 oz.
- Honey 1 oz.
- Cinnamon powder 1 tsp.
- Pinch of salt
- Cashew nuts 2 oz.
- Cashew butter 1 oz.
- Plant protein powder 2 oz.
- Shredded coconut 1 tbsp.

Preparation Method
1. At first, combine flax and melted butter in a large bowl. Add cinnamon, salt and honey, cashew butter, protein powder and mix well.
2. Add chopped cashews and mix everything evenly. Pour parchment paper into a casserole dish and spread the dough in a flat layer. Sprinkle crushed coconut and cinnamon up for beautiful crispy flavor.
3. Place them in a refrigerator and cool for 3 hours (night will give the best result). Cut into bars and enjoy the taste.

Nutritional Information
- Preparation Time:15 minutes
- Total servings: 8
- Calories: 119.5 (per serving)
- Fat: 3.2g
- Protein: 8.3g
- Carbs: 14.6g

Recipe 43: Grilled Chard

Ingredients
- Chard leaves 30
- Vegetable oil 3 tbsp.
- Vinegar 1 tbsp.
- Fresh thyme 1 tsp.
- Fresh lemon grass 1 tsp.
- Garlic cloves 3

Preparation Method
1. At first, preheat the oven to 400F. I like 10 chard leaves per person, depending on their size. Cut both ends and peel back the first or second layer of leaves and discard. Leave the chard in a pan with boiling salt water for 2 minutes.
2. Drain well and place in a bowl of vegetable oil, vinegar, chopped lemon grass, thyme and garlic. Spread the chard in a layer in a baking tray and bake for 10 minutes until it is caramelized.

Nutritional Information
- Preparation Time: 15 minutes
- Total servings: 3
- Calories: 59 (10 kale leaves per serving)
- Fat: 0.5g
- Protein: 2.1g
- Carbs: 9.3g

Recipe 44: Cabbage Biscuits

Ingredients
- Almond flour 1 ½ cup
- Cabbage 1.5 lb.
- Vegetable oil 2 oz.
- Ginger powder 1 tsp.
- Baking soda ½ tsp.
- Chopped walnuts 2 tbsp.
- Himalayan salt to taste

Preparation Method
1. At first, preheat your oven to 375F, blend cabbage until it is finely chopped.
2. In a large bowl, mix almond flour, salt, peppers, ginger powder, baking soda. Mix it well and add vegetable oil. Mix until a dough forms.
3. Add your cabbage to the mixture. Combine everything with your hands. Place your non-stick silpat on a cookie sheet, so that they do not stick as they boil. Form pies from the dough and sprinkle chopped walnuts. Bake like biscuits for 15 minutes or until they begin to flatten.
4. Turn it and continue baking for about 5 minutes then, turn your oven to roast and brew the biscuits for 3 minutes. Let it cool for 2 minutes before you enjoy the taste.

Nutritional Information
- Preparation Time: 30 minutes
- Total servings: 12
- Calories: 101 (per serving)
- Fat: 1.8g
- Protein: 5g
- Carbs: 13g

Recipe 45: Crunchy Chia Biscuits

Ingredients
- Chia flour 1 ½ cup
- Vegetable butter 2 oz.
- Baking soda ½ tsp.
- Cayenne pepper ¼ tsp.
- Garlic powder 1 tsp.
- Ginger powder 1 tsp.
- Thyme 2 tbsp.
- Pink salt to taste

Preparation Method
1. At first, preheat oven to 325F. Place a cookie sheet with parchment paper.
2. In a medium bowl, mix chia flour, pepper, salt and baking powder.
3. Add thyme, cayenne and garlic, ginger and stir until uniformly combined. Next, add to the pesto and snow bake until the dough forms into coarse crumbs.
4. Put the vegetable butter into the cracker mixture with a fork until the dough forms a ball.
5. Transfer the dough to the prepared cookie sheet and spread the dough thinly until it is about 1 mm thick. Make sure the thickness is the same, so that the biscuits evenly bake.
6. Place the pan in the pre-heated oven then sprinkle thyme over it and bake for 15 minutes to light golden-brown color. After baking, remove from the oven and cut into biscuits of the desired size.

Nutritional Information
- Preparation Time: 25 minutes
- Total servings: 6
- Calories: 88 (per serving)
- Fat: 1g
- Protein: 4.3g
- Carbs: 12.5g

Smoothie Recipes

Recipe 46: Coconut Chia Smoothies

Ingredients

- Frozen blueberries 4 oz.
- Coconut cream 2 oz.
- Almond milk 1 ½ cup
- Coconut oil 1 oz.
- Ground chia seed 1 oz.
- Sugar 1 oz.
- Cinnamon topping to taste

Preparation Method

- In blender, place all ingredients and blend on medium speed or until smooth
- Pour into serving glass and enjoy the taste

Nutritional Information

- Preparation Time: 5 minutes
- Total servings: 3
- Calories: 249 (per serving)
- Fat: 4.7g
- Protein: 6.2g
- Carbs: 17.7g

Recipe 47: Choco Avocado Smoothie

Ingredients
- Cashew milk 2 cups
- Avocado 3 oz.
- Frozen raspberries 2 oz.
- Cocoa powder 1 tbsp.
- Powdered Swerve 1 tbsp.
- Raspberry extract 5 drops

Preparation Method
- In blender, place all ingredients and blend on medium speed or until smooth
- Pour into serving glass and enjoy the taste

Nutritional Information
- Preparation Time: 5 minutes
- Total servings: 2
- Calories: 133 (per serving)
- Fat: 3.5g
- Protein: 6.1g
- Carbs: 12.8g

Recipe 48: Roman Green Smoothie

Ingredients
- Water 3 cups
- Romaine lettuce 5 oz.
- Fresh pineapple 2 oz.
- Fresh parsley 1 oz.
- Fresh ginger 1 tbsp.
- Cucumber 3 oz.
- Kiwi 3 oz.
- Avocado 2 oz.
- Granulated sugar 1 tbsp.

Preparation Method
- In blender, place all ingredients and blend on medium speed or until smooth
- Pour into serving glass and enjoy the taste

Nutritional Information
- Preparation Time: 5 minutes
- Total servings: 2
- Calories: 60 (per serving)
- Fat: 1.5g
- Protein: 3.3g
- Carbs: 13g

Recipe 49: Coconut Protein Smoothie

Ingredients

- Avocado 3 oz.
- Coconut milk ½ cup
- Fresh baby spinach 2 oz.
- Fresh mint 5 leaves
- Pistachio nuts 1 tbsp.
- Vanilla extract 1 tsp.
- Plant protein powder 1 tbsp.
- Stevia 3 drops
- Water 1 cup
- Ice cubes (if needed)

Preparation Method

- In blender, place all ingredients and blend on medium speed or until smooth
- Pour into serving glass and enjoy the taste

Nutritional Information

- Preparation Time: 5 minutes
- Total servings: 2
- Calories: 123 (per serving)
- Fat: 3.1g
- Protein: 7.2g
- Carbs: 12.4g

Recipe 50: Tropical Smoothie

Ingredients
- Ice cubes 7
- Coconut milk ½ cup
- Golden flaxseed meal 1 oz.
- Mango 1 oz.
- Guava juice ½ cup
- Lemon leaves 4
- Coconut oil 1 tbsp.
- Liquid stevia 20 drops
- Mango extract ½ tsp.
- Blueberry extract ½ tsp.

Preparation Method
1. In blender, place all ingredients and blend on medium speed or until smooth
2. Pour into serving glass and enjoy the taste

Nutritional Information
- Preparation Time: 5 minutes
- Total servings: 2
- Calories: 152 (per serving)
- Fat: 2g
- Protein: 5g
- Carbs: 14g

CONCLUSION

The PLANT-BASED DIET is the key to your success to achieve your dream in the right way but in short time. This book offers high energizing information, including nutritional recipes with fully packed vitamins, minerals, antioxidants and phytochemicals to the body. Overall benefits that you are going to get from the plant-based diet are:

- Acne control
- Decreasing heartburn
- Decreasing migraine attacks
- Decreasing sugar cravings
- Rapid weight loss
- Type 2 diabetes reversed
- Increased mental focus
- Improved physical endurance
- Metabolic syndrome
- Decreasing cancers
- Controlled blood pressure
- Less stomach problems

-- *[Tupakula]*

Manufactured by Amazon.ca
Bolton, ON

10911931R00039